It's All About Ewe

Celebrating the Joys of Our Friendship

Text by Rose Mary Harris

Artwork by Julie Sawyer

HARVEST HOUSE PUBLISHERS

EUGENE, OREGON

Published by Harvest House Publishers
Eugene, Oregon 97402
www.harvesthousepublishers.com

ISBN 0-7369-1307-6

Design and production by Garborg Design Works, Minneapolis, Minnesota

Printed in China.

04 05 06 07 08 09 10 11 12 / LP / 10 9 8 7 6 5 4 3 2 1

You Are Woolly Special!
With Blessings,
Two are better than one...If one falls down, his friend can help him up.
ECCLESIASTES 4:9-10

There I was thinking of heavenly blessings...

Take a good look at
God's wonders—they'll
take your breath away.

PSALM 66:5 THE MESSAGE

I'm thinking of you today in
your current surroundings—

Jesus' hands!

My sheep listen to My voice; I know them, and they follow Me...no one can snatch them out of My hand.

JOHN 10:27-28

You'll never know
how many times the
Lord has used you...

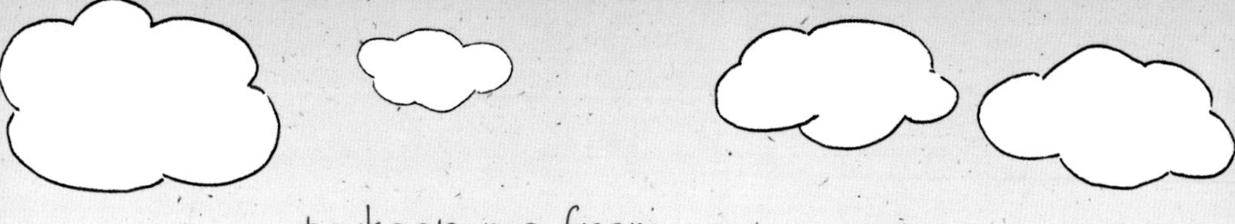

to keep me from
really unraveling!

Thank you from the
bottom of my heart.

He will not
forget your
work and the
love you
have shown
him as you
have helped
his people....

HEBREWS 6:10

Friends are necessary to a happy life.

HARRY EMERSON FOSDICK

I didn't find my friends; the good God gave them to me.

RALPH WALDO EMERSON

I love you not only for what you are,

It is my joy in life to find
At every turning of the road
The strong arm of a comrade kind
To help me onward with my load.

And since I have no gold to give,
And love alone must make amends,
My only prayer is, while I live—
God make me worthy of my friends.

FRANK DEMPSTER SHERMAN

but for what I am when I am with you.

ELIZABETH BARRETT BROWNING

I'm not sure what to do,
I'm not sure what to say...

But one thing's for sure—
I promise to pray!

For the eyes of the Lord are on the righteous
and his ears are attentive to their prayer...

1 PETER 3:12

Here...let me help you with that.

We'll just take it to Jesus in prayer.

Bear ye one another's burdens...

GALATIANS 6:2 KJV

I miss...

...your face!

I hope to see you soon, and we will talk face to face....

3 JOHN 1:14

Blek!

No matter how
yucky you feel...

...the Shepherd's love is very real!

I'm asking Him to hold you extra close these days.

As a shepherd looks after his scattered flock when he is with them, so will I look after my sheep.

EZEKIEL 34:12

Silences make the
real conversations
between friends.
Not the saying
but the never
needing to say
is what counts.

MARGARET LEE RUNBECK

Few delights can equal the mere
presence of one whom we trust utterly.

GEORGE MACDONALD

Someone has said, "If you want your friends to remember you, borrow something from them." I want to turn this around and say, if you want to remember your friends, be sure to borrow from them. Borrow faith, hope, and love. Borrow courage, humility, and integrity. Borrow their Christian example of the unseen values of the soul. Borrow their confidence in the living God and their loyalty to the triumphant Christ. Then indeed your days will be filled with strength.

JOHN W. MCKELVEY

Thinking of you...

...that's what the Shepherd and I love to do!

How precious it is, Lord, to realize that you are thinking about me constantly!

PSALM 139:17 TLB

What a friend
we have in Jesus...

...and what a friend
I have in you!

And he was called God's friend.

JAMES 2:23

You can always trust...

...your Shepherd!

May the God of hope fill you with all joy and peace as you trust in him...

ROMANS 15:13

The pasture is a better place...

...because you're here!

Thanking the Shepherd for you...

I thank my God every time I remember you.

PHILIPPIANS 1:3

So long as we love, we serve; so long as we are loved by others, I should say that we are almost indispensable; and no man is useless while he has a friend.

ROBERT LOUIS STEVENSON

was by the trail he left behind him.

HARRY LAUDER

Blessed are those who can give without remembering and take without forgetting.

ELIZABETH BIBESCO

My friends have made the story of my life. In a thousand ways they have turned my limitations into beautiful privileges, and enabled me to walk serene and happy in the shadow cast by my deprivation.

HELEN KELLER

god's incredible goodness...

The light of the righteous shines brightly.

PROVERBS 13:9

Thanks...

for going to such great heights in serving the Shepherd...
and
others!
I tell you the truth, whatever you did for one of the least of these brothers of mine, you did for me.
MATTHEW 25:40

A prayer...

...is an answer just
waiting to happen!
Isn't our God good?!

I love the Lord, for he heard my
voice...Because he turned his ear to me,
I will call on him as long as I live.

PSALM 116:1-2

You...

...are so special—
to the
Shepherd
and to me!

Every time you cross my mind, I break out in exclamations of thanks to God.

PHILIPPIANS 1:3 THE MESSAGE

There was a definite process by which one made people into friends; it involved talking to them and listening to them for hours at a time.

REBECCA WEST

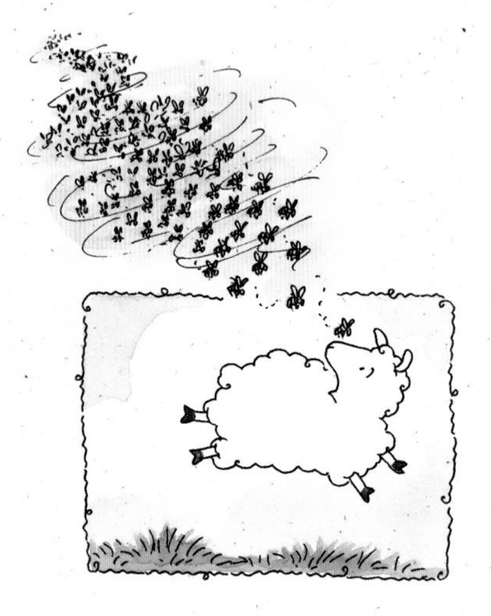

The finest thing of all about friendship is that it sends a ray of good hope into the future, and keeps our hearts from faltering or falling to the wayside.

CICERO

One can never speak enough of the virtues, the dangers, the power of shared laughter.

FRANÇOISE SAGAN

I love you because you have done more than any creed could have done to make me good, and more than any fate could have done to make me happy. You have done it without a touch, without a word, without a sign. You have done it by being yourself. Perhaps that is what being a friend means after all.

ROY CROFT

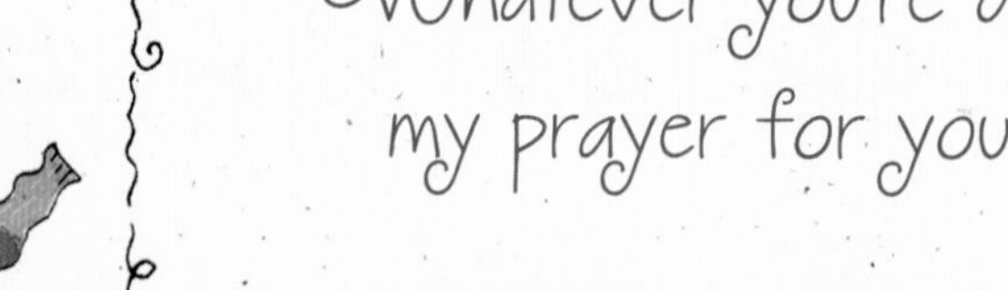

Whatever you're doing today,
my prayer for you is this—

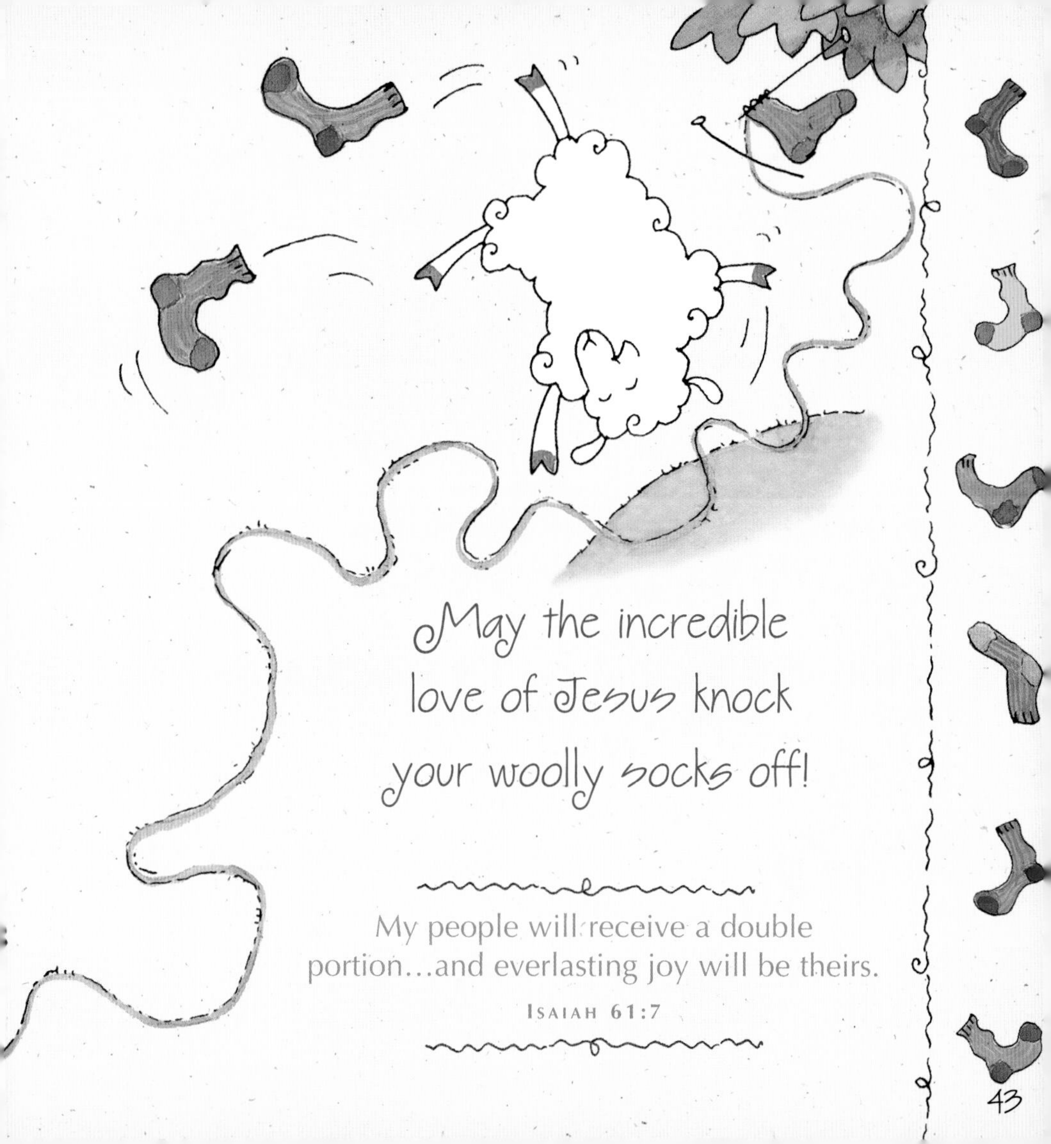

May the incredible love of Jesus knock your woolly socks off!

My people will receive a double portion…and everlasting joy will be theirs.

ISAIAH 61:7

Special Meeting
In Progress—
Just for you!

Hi—Just the Shepherd and me here, sharing one of our prayer closet joys—You.

When you pray, go into your room, close the door and pray to your Father...

MATTHEW 6:6

Bad hair day?

Don't worry—

God promises to make the rough places smooth.

I will turn
the darkness
into light
before them
and make the
rough places
smooth.
These are
the things
I will do.

ISAIAH 42:16

You've been on my mind...

May God...show you his kindness and mercy and give you great peace of heart and mind.

1 TIMOTHY 1:2 TLB

...and in my heart!

Long friendships are like jewels—polished over time to become beautiful and enduring.

CELIA BRAYFIELD

We've been friends forever.
I suppose that can't be true.
There must have been a time
before we became friends but
I can't remember it. You are in
my first memory and all my
best memories ever since.

LINDA MACFARLANE

Friendship hath the skill and observance of the best physician; the diligence and vigilance of the best nurse; and the tenderness and patience of the best mother.

LORD CLARENDON

I with you, and you with me,
Miles are short with company.
GEORGE ELIOT

No stain, no gain!

Been so glad to

be on my knees for you.

He answered their prayers,
because they trusted in Him.

1 CHRONICLES 5:20

Been smiling all day...

...'cause you and our Shepherd have been on my mind!

Every time I think of you—and I think of you often!—I thank God for you....

1 CORINTHIANS 1:4 THE MESSAGE

Thought you might need a little pick-me-up today...

Carry each
other's burdens,
and in this
way you will
fulfill the law
of Christ.

GALATIANS 6:2

...so I prayed for you.

Please open immediately!

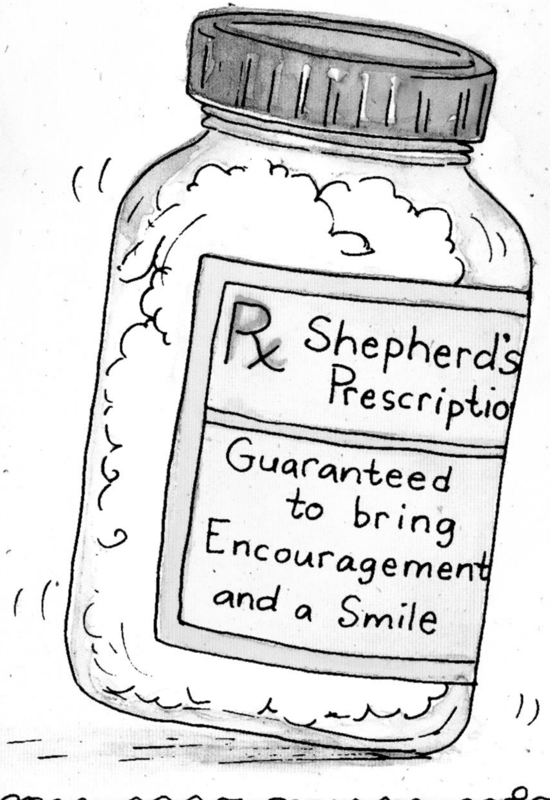

Rx Shepherd's
Prescriptio

Guaranteed
to bring
Encouragement
and a Smile

pop
boing
Hello!
Just wanted you to know
that I'm caring and praying!

I'll give you the best of care...

PSALM 91:14 THE MESSAGE

Do you have any idea...

...how much you mean to me?

In all my prayers for all of you, I always pray with joy because of your partnership in the gospel from the first day until now.

PHILIPPIANS 1:4-5

Friendships like ours...

And there shall
be one flock and
one Shepherd.

JOHN 10:16

...are developed by the
Shepherd Himself!

I have learned that to have a good friend
is the purest of all God's gifts, for it is
a love that has no exchange of payment.

FRANCES FARMER